CONQUEROR
How I lost 100 Pounds

JENNIFER E. SANTOS

Copyright © 2021
JENNIFER E. SANTOS
CONQUEROR
How I lost 100 Pounds
All rights reserved.

No part of this publication may be reproduced, distributed, or transmitted in any form or by any means, including photocopying, recording, or other electronic or mechanical methods, without the prior written permission of the publisher, except in the case of brief quotations embodied in critical reviews and certain other non-commercial uses permitted by copyright law.

JENNIFER E. SANTOS

Printed in the United States of America
First Printing 2021
First Edition 2021

10 9 8 7 6 5 4 3 2 1

CONQUEROR

Table of Contents

Dedication 1

Introduction 3

Chapter 1 9

Love

Chapter 2 17

Discipline

Chapter 3 23

ME VS. ME

Chapter 4 29

You Cannot Outrun Your Mouth

Chapter 5 39

Enjoy the Journey

Conclusion 45

Have Faith

Dedication

This book is dedicated to everyone who struggles with weight issues and low self-worth. In society we are judged heavily upon appearance and what is considered aesthetically pleasing in the "eyes of man." From tv, print, radio, and social media, we are bombarded with images that are designed to influence us to look and act a certain way. To be very honest, I constantly compared myself to these images and desperately tried to appear that way. I questioned everything from my dark skin tone, my natural hair texture, my big hips and lips.

Even at 148 pounds in the military I struggled with low self-esteem issues. I wanted to be accepted and constantly felt like I could never measure up to people and their expectations of me. Feeling like I had no voice, I battled feelings of low self-worth and depression and I turned to my drug of choice. I used food and sugar to deal with life and got up over 320 lbs. I truly thank God who gave me the strength and courage to stand up for myself and face my fears. To believe Him that I am loved. A love so strong that says I am worth it. I was worth His life. That is the price He paid so that I could have mine. You are worth it! You are loved. No matter what size you are or the struggles you may face, you are worthy of God's love.

In this book, I will share how God's word helped me to lose weight and become who he called me to be. It is not about the weight. It is a matter of the heart. What do you think of yourself and what you are capable of—what hidden potential that is buried deep within you and is meant to be released as a gift to the world. But it is bogged down with negative mindsets and destructive behaviors that are meant to keep you from being all that God has destined you to be. I wholeheartedly believe that if you can conquer your mind, you will conquer your life. Are you ready to change your life? Let's go, Conqueror!

Introduction

As a child and teenager, I was in great shape. I was very athletic. I ran track, played volleyball, danced, and I loved roller-skating around the neighborhood. I was happy. But as a child, I was made fun of for having big lips and I experienced being bullied and jumped everyday walking home from school. In all honesty, I did not let that slow me down. Although I was highly active, my eating habits were not the best. I would eat copious amounts of foods in one sitting. To this day, I can remember someone saying to me "Girl, you eat a lot!" and I was proud of that. I could consume enormous quantities of food and it did not affect my size. I was young and carefree and did not care about my decisions at times. It was not until I got into high school that I started hanging with the wrong crowd. At that age, I was heavily influenced by what I saw and I imitated it. I wanted to be like those desirable women featured in the music, videos, and movies.

I grew up with Christian values, but I lost my virginity at the age of 16. I never heard from that boy again. From that point onward, the amount of guilt and shame I carried began to erode my self-confidence. With one bad decision after the next, I searched for love and acceptance. Everyone knew about my past, and I wanted to prove that I was good enough. That I was honorable. So, when I was 18, I joined the Air Force.

Having my athletic background, I was able to do well in the Air Force. It was a culture shock, but I adjusted to military life. I started making friends and a little money and was able to achieve the things I wanted. But I still struggled with feelings of inadequacy and low self-worth. You see, on the outside I became an expert at appearing happy, but I was shy and angry. Angry for losing the one thing I thought made me special. Angry at myself for feeling like I could never measure up to people and society's expectations of what is considered "beauty" and having "success."

CONQUEROR

Being in the military gave me a sense of acceptance, but I was still making bad decisions. By the time I was a few years in, I had two kids, and I was a single parent. I was extremely grateful for my children. They gave me the strength and purpose to turn my life around and make good decisions. I was happy, but it was fleeting. To be honest, I was struggling. I was constantly trying to prove that I was special. I had to be perfect. Over the years, my weight slowly crept up.

My eating habits never changed, and I consumed enormous amounts of pizza, Chinese food, and pints of ice-cream. Once again, I relied on athletics to keep me in the Air Force. So, I worked out diligently to meet expectations. I was diagnosed with depression and I did my best at the time to be there for my family. On a remote assignment across the world, separated from the one thing that kept me going, my children, I was broken and tried to commit suicide. It was one of the darkest seasons of my life, but it was during this time that I met my wonderful husband. I always call him my knight in shining armor. We met, became friends, and our friendship became a relationship and we got married. We traveled the world; we had more babies, and life was good. I had everything I wanted. A family.

I thought marriage would solve all my problems. I thought my husband would cure me, for me. What is wrong with me, I thought? How do I get out of these cycles of depression? I was happy for a few weeks and then went back to not feeling good enough. Only God could fix me, but I did not realize it then. Once again, I turned to food to cope.

Once I decided to leave the Air Force, my weight slowly started climbing. Every year I would gain about 20 pounds. Then, one day, I tipped the scales at over 320 pounds. All those years of eating what I wanted when I wanted, without any concern for my future caught up with me. How did I get there? Here I was this bright, young girl, full of potential and I would have never imagined being here. I tried many diets hoping to lose weight quickly, and it never worked. I spent money I did not have, bought programs that promised results and never provided real success. I never kept to a diet for more than a week.

CONQUEROR

Even though I had the desire to lose weight, I could not stop binging on food including large amounts sugar. I knew the consequences of eating this way, but deep in my heart I felt like I could not do otherwise. I knew I had a lot of weight to lose, but it seemed impossible. I tried and tried to no avail. I bought every fitness DVD program and diet known to man, and nothing. So, I started to accept the fact that I would remain at that size. I let life pass me by. I was afraid of facing my fears. The weight was just a deeper issue of what was going on in my heart and mind. I was trying to please man and prove my worth to others.

I had the desire to make a change and finally lose the weight. I fell down the stairs of my home and broke my ankle and one year later, I sprained my right knee. All my life, I'd never had broken bones, and this happened right when I got serious about my health. At the doctor's appointment as he was examining my knee, with brutal honesty he said, "You know, you are just really heavy." In that moment, I felt defeated.

When I got home, I made a journal entry.

Apr 22, 2020

OBESITY IS DEAD TO ME!

I put the notebook down and looked in the mirror and asked myself, "What happened?" With tears streaming down my eyes, I began crying out to God!

Chapter 1

Love

As I cried out to God for help, I remember feeling so weak and helpless. Over 320 pounds with a stiff ankle and a sprained knee. I was in a lot of pain. This weight was holding me back from having the life I genuinely wanted. So many questions and feelings of self-doubt flooded my mind. Thoughts like, "You can't do this," and "Where do I start?" and "You'll always be this way. Just accept it," This is your life now! However, amid the chaos of my negative self-talk, I came to the realization that I was making excuses. I needed to be accountable for my life and the decisions I made to get me to this point. I was tired of playing the blame game. I was desperate for change. I turned to the only one who could help me out of this vicious cycle.

3 John 1:2 KJV "Beloved, I wish above all things that thou mayest prosper and be in health, even as thy soul prospers." As I began to read and meditate on this scripture every day, Father God was showing me that number one, I am loved. Let us stop right there. God calls me his child. All I ever wanted was to be loved. No conditions, no expectations, period. I do not have to jump through hoops to obtain his love and affection. His love is unconditional. He is very intentional about His word. He accepts me for who I am, and I do not have to compromise myself in any way to be loved. His love motivates me to become the person He said I could be. His love shows me that my destructive vices are not of Him, and that it is not me, so I can change. He is a good father, and he expresses his love to his children through word and deed. He demonstrated his love by dying on the cross, so that I could have life. So, as His child, I must be very intentional about my words and actions. God's love must be the foundation of how I think. Like Christ, I must pick up my cross and deny myself. I must make some sacrifices. Easier said than done, right? To bring about my Father's will on this Earth, I must be

intentional about how I live my life and how I treat myself and others around me.

I must know that I am loved, and my actions must correspond. He called me beloved. I am not abandoned, a victim, crazy, ugly, mediocre, unsuccessful, and worthless! I am beloved. In that moment I started realizing that in my heart and mind I was struggling with low self-worth. I let lies and negative words brew in my heart. Other people and I myself spoke these lies over the course of my lifetime. I let those negative words influence my mind. Because I believed these words to be true, I became what I repeated. (Proverbs 23:7). So, I had to shift my focus off of myself and believe in my heart that I am loved by God. If everything was stripped from me—the approval of man, degrees, success, material possessions, good looks, and the list goes on and on down to the lowest common denominator—who am I? What do I have? What makes me valuable?

I have the love of God, and his love is all I need. Because of His love, I have so much to offer this world. I must be rooted in the truth of his love because how I think about myself will form the decisions that lead to daily habits that form the very essence of who I am and what I become. He loves you too. No conditions. He wants us to prosper physically and mentally, and to have health in every area of life. This way of thinking is a lifestyle. God wants us to flourish and fly higher than we could ever imagine. He wants our souls to prosper. He cares how we think, how we feel, and He wants us to have the will to live. He wants us to flourish. He wants us to have success, but we must believe. That was my problem. I was not believing.

I always approached losing weight and getting healthy as something that I could never do. Yes, I had all this weight to lose and it seemed impossible. As with any other goal I wanted to accomplish, when the going got tough, I gave up. I feared failing and having people's disapproval. You cannot live that way.

My mindset shifted. Because of God's love I have health. I will prosper and succeed. Armed with the knowledge of God's word, I felt such a strength and zeal for life. I realized it was my fault; I was holding myself back this whole time. I was making excuses and being prideful. I wanted what I wanted, not understanding that every action we take has a good consequence or a bad consequence.

CONQUEROR

My mind was made up. As I meditated on God's love, I knew if I wanted to prosper, my lifestyle had to change. Romans 8: 37 KJV: "Nay, in all these things we are more than conquerors through him that loved us."

Conqueror Lifestyle

A conqueror is defined as someone who overcomes an adversary. Jesus is my conquering King who defeated my enemy at the cross. Because of my faith in him, I conquer all my enemies, meaning negative mindsets and concepts that speak contrary to the truth of God's word. We do not conquer people. That's not God's nature. We love like he loves us. It is about conquering erroneous belief systems that would keep us in bondage and prevent us from prospering in life. I was using food and sugar to deal with feelings of low self-worth. I knew it was wrong, but I could not stop the binges. A form of self-abuse led me down a path of destruction.

Life is beautiful, but it is hard sometimes. However, I cannot let the issues of life and my emotions drive me to make decisions that would end my life prematurely.

I must take the mindset of a conqueror. And you too are a conqueror. Because that is who God says we are. It is not just a weight loss journey. Thinking this way becomes a way of life. A conqueror lifestyle.

CONQUEROR

No matter the obstacle that may stand in the way. We have overwhelming victory. We must go into the battle knowing we have the victory. If you can conquer your mind, you will conquer your life.

Chapter 2
Discipline

In November 2019, I remember sitting having my daily devotional, and I wrote in my journal, "Father God told me that 2020 would be the year of discipline for me." At the time I was like, Okay, Lord am I hearing you correctly? But it was the very truth.

On April 22, 2020, I started my journey, and I soon realized that I must become acquainted with the concept of discipline. To be honest with you, I was scared. I liked my comfort and the familiar. I knew I had to eat right, but I did not want to, and look where that got me. Sick and Tired. Quickly, it became a matter of life and death. Discipline is doing what needs to be done, even when you do not feel like it. I call it practicing delayed gratification or exercising self-control. Delayed does not mean never, just not right now. We live in a time of instant gratification. I must have it now at all cost, regardless of the consequences. I was borrowing against my life, and payment was due!

Practicing delayed gratification is a principle that I live by. If I wanted to be free of this weight and reclaim my health, I had to keep my eyes focused on God's word concerning my health and I needed to tell myself *no!* I must endure so that later I could have freedom.

Proverbs 29:18 KJV, "Where there is no vision, the people perish." I started to understand that every day God's word gave me a vision concerning my health, and that vision was more important than what I wanted. Having this mindset gave me the strength I needed to practice self-control in my daily eating habits. There were days I wanted to give up. It seemed impossible. But I would visualize myself being healthy and prosperous. I had to trust God and trust the process. I learned that keeping my eyes focused on my vision—practicing discipline and consistency—would lead me to victory. Every day we must choose to do those things that we know are good for us, like eating right, exercising, meditation, etc.

CONQUEROR

Even, when we do not feel like it. That is when growth will happen. It is easy to give in to desire and temptation. It is much harder to say no. Self-control is everything. Without it, life will quickly spin out of control. Through practicing discipline and self-control, good habits start to form.

Daily Habits

I was super pumped and motivated to lose the weight. After a week or two, I lost about 12 pounds. I was excited. But I hit plateaus and I would get discouraged. What kept me going were the good habits I started to form along the way and my vision. The habits we form daily shape who we become. Every day I practiced eating the same healthy meals. I kept it quite simple. That is what worked for me. Everyone must find what works best for them. I did not want to overly complicate things. I had a set schedule that I followed it every day. So, even when I encountered tough days, I followed my routine, and eventually the plateau would break.

It helped me to understand that I had a bad habit of giving up when things got tough. I would think, "Well, I had that slice of pizza, so my whole diet is messed up, and I'll just re-start on Monday. Then Monday would show up and nothing. I would keep postponing dieting until the following week. And I watched as another year came and went, as my health slowly declined. But even though I messed up during my journey, I refused to give up. That is the key. There will be times when we fall. It does not mean we are failures. Just get back up. Do not give up! Every day I woke up and looked in the mirror, and said, "This is my life." I'm not going to admit defeat. No matter what!

When I started my journey, I thought I had to make this huge overhaul of my diet and workout for ten hours. To be honest that did not work for me because it was not sustainable. I got overwhelmed. In the past, I would set my New Year's resolution, and come February I gave up and was feeling defeated. This time around, I decided I would take small steps.

For instance, I had to have something sweet after dinner every night, and I would eat it in bed. I knew this as my biggest issue, so I focused on that first. I ate my normal dinner, but I set a goal of no longer eating in bed at night and switched my sweets for my favorite fruit, watermelon.

I felt satisfied and I was happy because I was making changes towards my health but not depriving myself of my favorite foods. Because I made that slight change, I ended up losing a few pounds.

I was so excited. I saw how slight changes over time led me to conquer major obstacles. I never lost twenty pounds in two weeks. It would average two or three pounds a week. That is the power of discipline and I would build on each step. My confidence soared.

Chapter 3
ME VS. ME

As long as I could remember I had constantly compared myself to other people. If I had the same level of success or beauty that another person had, I felt great. If I did not, wow, I would become insecure and jealous to the point that I started living in a bubble and I was content with that. The hard truth is there will always be someone who has more money, success, and good looks. The issue was not them. It was me.

2 Corinthians 10:12 KJV "For we dare not make ourselves of the number or compare ourselves with some that commend themselves: but they are measuring themselves by themselves, and comparing themselves among themselves, are not wise."

During this journey I was standing face to face with the fears and insecurities that constantly led me to compare myself to others. The only measuring stick I should use was the cross. God's love and the truth of his word is how I should view myself. Comparing my life and accomplishments against other people is foolish. God created us unique and special in our own ways. It was my character that was lacking and needed to be developed. I understand that I cannot live for the approval of others. I felt silly and exhausted. I was tired of, "trying to prove my worth." I wanted freedom. I needed to stop trying. I needed to be the person God called me to be and not who society says I am.

MOVE FORWARD

I became super focused on the task at hand. I had complete tunnel vision. I decided to let go of the past. The race is not about anyone else, but the race is about becoming the person that God called me to be. Pursuing my purpose. I wanted to become the best version of myself. I wanted to move forward and never settling for mediocrity. I can be happy for people and celebrate their wins, without looking down on myself or thinking so highly of myself. I know that with God, in everything we do, it is to glorify Him. Our season will come. This attitude is a true sign of a secure person.

I had to get real with myself. It is a fact that I was bullied and abandoned by people that I thought had my back. I was lied to and talked about. I have experienced so much pain and anguish and I have caused pain and anguish in the lives of others as well. There were feelings of shame and guilt, but it was all excuses. I was allowing my pain to keep me from having the life I genuinely wanted. I feared people, but I was afraid of myself. At one of the darkest moments of my life, I decided that this journey was about dealing with me.

This is your life. Fight for it. If not for you, then who? What about my future? My family? My children and their children? What legacy will I leave behind? It is time to move forward with my life because time waits for no man. It starts with me. Every day I woke up and made decisions that pushed me past my comfort zone. I pushed myself to be the absolute best. I competed against myself every day. I used pictures of myself from back in the day when I was slimmer and I competed against her. If I walked one mile one day, the next I would walk a mile and a half. Every day I made a conscience effort to push past my last barrier. The minute I took my eyes off people and put them on God and bettering myself, I started experiencing peace in my mind. I would tell myself, "Stop worrying about others and what they have going on and mind your business." Every day I watched as God began to transform my life. Slowly, I was climbing out of the pit of depression and comparison.

I was scared to face myself and the sacrifices it would require. But I am glad for the journey because it showed me the hidden potential that was deep within. I am grateful because with God all things are truly possible. I think back on all those dreams and goals I had, but I was too afraid to step out. It takes courage to face your fears and confront yourself.

By far this has been one of the toughest things I have ever had to do. But on the other side, there is joy and peace. You must know that with God on your side, you can conquer the world, but you must first conquer you. All the hidden potential that is placed inside of you must come forth. Sometimes, we judge a book by its cover.

If it does not look a certain way, people are disregarded like trash. But God is looking for the overlooked, discarded, abandoned, and oppressed. He recovers them and shows them that how you started has no bearing on your future. It is not over!

Chapter 4

You Cannot Outrun Your Mouth

I constantly told myself, "J, you can't outrun your mouth." What I meant is that in the past, I always had the mentality of you can eat what you want, just workout. Now, that works for some people, but not me. I had a huge problem with binge eating. I did not understand the concept of a serving size. I had to have the whole pint of ice cream. I would foolishly wake up after a night of binging and do some cardio training, thinking it would erase the damage caused by my crazy eating habits. It did not change anything, and I tipped the scales at over 320 pounds. I do not care how much you run; if you are eating more calories than your body requires, you will gain weight. I quickly learned that weight loss starts in the kitchen. If I wanted to change and reclaim my health, I had to start doing things differently.

There was so much information out there about the best diets. Jenny Craig, Nutrisystem. I mean the list is endless. I tried it all, but I could not stick with it. I had to find something that worked for me. Find something that works for you and stick with it. I decided that I would eliminate the biggest culprit for me which was fried food. Honey, I loved anything fried, especially fried chicken. It was one of my favorite foods. I ate it daily for years.

I then eliminated all processed and sugary drinks. That was by far, one of the toughest things I had to do. I was trying to break unhealthy habits. I could see how consuming too much processed foods and sugary drinks over time got me to where I was. Initially, I often had cravings. I was extremely irritable because my body was used to having sugar and salt. I was going through withdrawal.

Amid the withdrawal, we were going through a pandemic and were placed on lock-down. In thirty-five years of living on this earth, I had never experienced anything like this. There was such hysteria and fear in the air, and rightfully so. The uncertainty of it all. Every time I turned on the news, death tolls were rising, people were losing their jobs and homes and businesses; you could feel the tension in the air. I just wanted to give in. It was such an extremely stressful time. My husband was in the medical field, so he was essential personnel, worked twelve hours a day, and came home to help me homeschool our five children. I thanked God for him. I was worried about him going outside, but he would say, "Babe, don't worry. I am in the Father's hands." He was right and that was what we stood on. My husband was my rock. He was my support system during this time. In the past, I would have turned to food and sweets to help me cope, but I could not give in. I did not want food and sugar to have power over me.

FASTING

When the children were situated for school, I took my Bible, notepad, and a glass of ginger tea and sat on my front porch. I decided I would fast and eat one meal a day. Now, I know that seems extreme, but I had to get away from my crutches and vices. I had gotten so used to all the noise that it became a distraction. I turned off the news, got off my phone, pushed my plate away, and sat alone with my thoughts and focused my mind on God's love for me. I was tired of the rat race. I wanted peace. True peace in my mind.

Isaiah 26:3 KJV "Thou wilt keep him in perfect peace, whose mind is stayed on thee: because he trusted in thee."

Jesus is my peace. Sitting on that porch he was teaching me that to have peace in my mind, it must come from Him. I was looking at the wrong things. I was searching for peace and comfort in food and sugar and the approval of people. I did not even realize it. When I got good news, I automatically ate. When there was sad news, or some sort of problem, I ate. I would experience temporary peace, but it could never truly comfort me. I was seeking security. I worshipped food. It became an idol. Fasting helped me to see that all I needed was God. He is my peace and security. If I have him, I will be okay. Yes, life hurts sometimes, but I must deal with my emotions in a healthy way. I realized that I did not need as much food. Slowly, I gained confidence and trust in God's word.

Every day during the pandemic, I fasted until 5 or 6 pm. It was hard, but it helped me shift my mindset. I couldn't let anything have power over my life to the point that it was taking the place of Christ. The addictions and cravings began to break. I felt true peace and freedom, the things I thought I could not have. With God, I did it. When it was time for me to eat, all I wanted was healthy food.

I started eating foods like broccoli, cucumber salads, and fish. I developed a love for cruciferous vegetables. I loved making big salads filled with green lettuce, onions, and cheese. Even though I started watching my carb intake, I still ate low sugar oatmeal, apples with peanut butter, and lots of watermelon. In the beginning of my journey, I ate baked chicken and lots of fish, including wild caught salmon, scallops and tuna. Healthy eating was not so bad. I used many different herbs, seasonings, and spices, including salt and it was delicious.

I thoroughly enjoyed my one meal a day. I started understanding that my body was God's temple, and I must be a good steward of what He gives me.

80/20 RULE

In the past when there was fast food around, I would give in and eat and feel horrible right afterward. Now, I can look at it, and stand firm. If I want to have something, I do, and if I don't, I am good either way. But fasting helped me with self-control. You must practice it. A quality of a great leader is self-control. I had to lead myself. So, I decided on the 80/20 rule. It means 80 percent of the time I eat healthy, whole unprocessed foods. And the other 20 percent of the time, I have my cheat meals. It is not even a cheat meal. It is just learning how to be balanced. I decided early on in my journey that I could not have entire days of eating junk food. In the past, having a whole day of eating junk food would lead to binges. So, I told myself that you get a cheat meal and one desert of your choice. For me, this was perfect.

For my cheat meals, I would eat things like fried chicken, pizza, and my favorite candy bars, Reese's Pieces. It felt great to be able to have my meal and just move on. For me there are still some parameters that I set around my "cheat meals." For example, I do not drink my calories. I was heavily addicted to sugary drinks. I drank upwards of four cans of soda a day. That was not optimal for my health. It was habit. Every time I consumed food, I had to have a sugary beverage. Now, I drink only water and I do not miss the sugary drinks. This is just me. At the end of the day, we all must make decisions that are best for our lives. What works for you, may not work for me. The key is to listen to your body.

I started becoming extremely sensitive to my body and how certain foods affected me. For instance, when I cut out the sugary drinks, I noticed I did not have as much joint pain and stiffness. I noticed I was becoming more flexible, experienced mental clarity, and razor-sharp focus. I became energetic and wanted to work out harder and play outside with my children. I wanted to be active and productive. God created us to be fruitful. We are made in His image. We are to create and produce things. Shifting my focus from food allowed me to put my time and energy into the gifts and talents that God gave me. I started writing more, giving myself to the creative process.

CONQUEROR

As I progressed in my journey, I did not need the 20% as much. Now, I can go a month or so and I am okay. It is a new way of life and thinking. We must continue to make strides towards our goals but enjoy life.

Chapter 5
Enjoy the Journey

When I first started my journey toward health, I thought I was going to be miserable. But as it turned out, it has been the most rewarding experience of my life. We all like a challenge, and every day I was waking up seeing how much I was changing. Not only on the outside, but inside. I watched as God was showing me the very thing, I was afraid of—failure. His love stands by my side and speaks to every fear. Although, I am not at my "ideal" size or weight, I am joyful for where I am now, and I see that it is a process. In the past, I had thoughts like, "Once I lose the weight, I'll be happy." But my joyfulness cannot depend upon people and things. It is no one's responsibility to make me happy. In life there will be disappointment, but true joy can only come from Him. I sincerely believe that even if we have a billion dollars, wear a size 0 and possess everything we want in life, we may still be unhappy. Look at all the billionaires and millionaires in the world who have everything at their disposal, but end up committing suicide.

1 Timothy 6:6 KJV "But Godliness with contentment is great gain."

True contentment can only come from God. I had to learn this and practice it. I took my eyes off all the things I did not have and placed my eyes on Him. I became grateful for the life he gives. Instead of looking down on myself for not having what is considered "success" in the world's system—whatever it is—I look up to Him. If you have God, you have true wealth. No amount of money, power, and sex can compare to Him. I wanted to seek Him. Everything else pales in comparison. I had wasted time chasing after things that I thought would make me happy and successful. He is life itself. True success and happiness are walking in the purpose we were created for. I love helping and encouraging people. If my journey can help someone else, then I am most fulfilled and content.

CONQUEROR

Embarking on this journey, I started seeing positive ripple effects in other areas of my life.

No matter what, there will always be some problem to overcome. Life will never be perfect. I decided to start living now and be joyful for the one true love I have. He will give us the joy we need to endure the journey and live a life of prosperity and contentment.

Patience

The beautiful thing about life is the opportunity to become all that God has destined us to be. I have learned that a person must continue to grow and flourish—to go beyond the limitations that we place on ourselves—to break through veils of lies and mindsets that keep us in bondage. Anything worth having will require a fight. It is not going to be easy. This journey requires patience. Do not rush the process. What lessons are you supposed to learn? How is this journey going to strengthen your character? How is it going to make you a better person?

In the beginning of my journey, I felt like I was racing against a clock. Although I had a lot of weight to lose, I was allowing fear to rush me outside of God's timing. I thought it had to happen in my timeframe, and if it did not, I was scared that it would never happen. God was teaching me patience. As children of God, He gives us so many wonderful promises. Most of us struggle in the time between the promise and the manifestation.

CONQUEROR

God promised Abraham that he would be the father of many nations. It seemed like the promise was not going to happen because Abraham and his wife, Sara were old. But God strengthened them to conceive and bring forth Isaac, ultimately birthing the twelve tribes of Israel, and from the tribe of Judah came forth the Messiah, Jesus the Christ and He brought forth salvation for the entire world. Be patient and wait for God's timing because you are going to bring forth a gift that will change the world.

Conclusion
Have Faith

On this journey called life, I am truly learning how to trust God. Trusting God means that I can no longer live in the past. I must trust God that I am healthy and whole. We must live with the vision that God gives us. We cannot live according to what we see because it is temporary. It may be a fact that we face medical issues, or circumstances hinder us on all sides. But we must develop such confidence in God and his ability that it causes us to change our minds about the obstacles we face. Having faith in his words gives us the boldness to defy the odds. It is a winning attitude. We are more than conquerors. So, it may look like I am defeated, but the truth is, I have overwhelming victory, and my circumstances do not reflect the truth of who I am and what I can become.

For me, losing 100 pounds is just the beginning. I no longer want to sit back and let life pass me by. People will always talk. There will always be critics and some obstacle to overcome. I cannot let that stop me. Let their words fall on deaf ears. Fly like an eagle. Defy the odds. Be the leader and roar like a lion. For so long I felt like I did not have a voice, and no one would listen to what I had to say, but that is a lie. God did not bring us through all that adversity for no reason. Being here now is a testament of God's love and grace that we are here for a purpose. What do you want? To stop drinking? Do it. To lose weight? Do it. To gain better health? Do it. To get out of debt? Do it. To break the addiction? Do it. To go back to school? Do it. To write the book? Do it. To start the business? Do it.

There is so much more out there, a world filled with endless possibilities. Having the right mindset is the foundation. We cannot live by what others say we are and their perception of us. God has given us gifts and talents that we must nurture, develop, and train to manifest who we are and what we give to the world. All your hopes and dreams can be realized, but you must believe that it can happen.

Life is so precious. No more wasting time. One of the most valuable resources we have on this earth is twenty-four hours. We all have the same twenty-four hours. What are you doing with your time to help you become the person you want to be? You must know that your time is precious. Do not waste it on activities or bad habits that will keep you from releasing your potential.

We have territory to claim. No more distractions. Get up and fight! There are lives to save and deliver. No more wasting time, wallowing in the pain and regret of yesteryear. Yes, we make mistakes. But it doesn't define who we are. Do not live in the past. Stop looking back. Your future is bright. Every day we have the opportunity from God to get up and be all that He said we are. To live a life that reflects the truth of His words. To live a life of freedom. No more limits. No more being trapped in vicious cycles of defeat. Believe God's words that you are victorious. Be who He called you to be and bring forth the gift that was placed inside of you. Be you. In the words of Apostle Paul, "The earth is awaiting the true manifestation of the Sons of God."